# CCI AND ANTI-COMPETITIVE BEHAVIOUR: STUDY OF THE GOOGLE INC CASE

## VOLUME 2, ISSUE 3 OF BRILLOPEDIA

SAHIL ALI

# Contents

# Preface

"Start writing, no matter what. The water does not flow until the faucet is turned on".

- Louis L'Amour

Hundreds of students and professors are contributing their work to Brillopedia, we are here to provide ample information about Law and Contemporary issues. Our aim is to provide a platform for today's generation to express their views and ideas on law and contemporary law.

# Author

Sahil Ali

# CHAPTER ONE

# ABSTRACT

The working of an organisation that plays a regulatory role can be best understood by grasping its on ground functioning. This paper hence makes an attempt the study the role and functioning of the Competition Commission of India with reference to a case study through a thorough analysis of the issues at hand, the arguments presented by both the sides and the conclusions drawn thereto. The Act of 2002, concerning the regulation of forces in the market and the protection of the interests of consumers from an unhinged manipulation of market prices and other predatory practices by those forces was the soul behind the establishment of the CCI, which now functions as the core body for the prevention of abuse of dominant position in market.

# CHAPTER TWO

# INTRODUCTION AND BACKGROUND

In this paper we the primary legislation that concerns us is the Competition Act of 2002.India's Competition Commission was constituted in compliance with the 2002 Act so as to facilitate and undertake the following functions :

(i) primarily to offer institutional assistance and prevent adverse effects on competition

(ii) encourage and maintain competition in market

(iii) safeguard consumer interests; and

(iv) guarantee the freedom of commerce practised by other market actors.

The CCI has been given sufficient authority to look into, stop, and punish anti-competitive behaviour. It can look into and outlaw anti-competitive agreements and the abuse of dominant positions on its own initiative after receiving information or following a government referral. Additionally, for combinations (acquisition, merger and amalgamation),The CCI may make inquiries based on information it has on hand or data supplied by the parties throughout the CCI's notification and approval process. It has a Director General who oversees investigations and has the authority to order the production of evidence, record sworn testimony, and launch dawn raids.

The CCI has the authority to issue temporary orders preventing parties from engaging in alleged anti-competitive behaviour while an investigation is ongoing. If the CCI determines that there has been a violation of a statutory restriction, it may, among other things, order the offending business to stop engaging in the unlawful behaviour, levy a fine, and issue additional orders as it sees fit.

Along with the aforementioned authority, the CCI can also mandate the division of a dominant enterprise to make sure it doesn't abuse its position as a dominant one. In the case of mergers, the CCI can approve, disapprove, or suggest changes to the proposed merger. The CCI also has the authority to take extraterritorial action against anti-competitive behaviour that occurs outside of India and has, or is expected to have, a significant negative impact on competition in India.

The CCI is given the authority to ensure regulatory observance and enforcement through the imposition of financial penalties. If a CCI order or direction is disobeyed, the CCI may fine the violator up to a maximum of 100 million rupees and up to 100,000 rupees per day of non-compliance.A punishment of up to 250 million rupees or both might be levied for failure to follow the directions given or the fine imposed by the CCI. Upto three years in prison or both as a form of punishment.

Penalties apply for failing to notify the CCI of a proposed combination that can reach a maximum of 1% of the combined assets or entire turnover, whichever is larger. In a similar vein, anyone involved in a combination who makes a false statement or omits to provide important information is responsible for 5 million rupees as a minimum fine and 10 million rupees as the maximum. A fine of up to 10 million rupees may be imposed on anyone found guilty of making a false statement, providing a false document, knowingly omitting to declare a material fact, modifying, suppressing, or destroying a material document. Anyone who can demonstrate a loss or injury brought on by an enterprise's anti-competitive behaviour or its inability to adhere to the instructions and guidelines of the CCI or Appellate Tribunal may seek compensation from the Appellate Tribunal.

# CHAPTER THREE

# SCOPE AND OBJECTIVE

The purpose and goals of an organisationlike CCI serve as a window of communication through which it can explain to the outside world why it exists and for whom.

Goal: To encourage firms to be ethical, competitive, and inventive while also improving consumer welfare and supporting economic growth through participation and enforcement.

The Competition Commission of India's objective is to create a healthy, competitive environment through: Proactive engagement with all stakeholders, including consumers, business, the government, and other international jurisdictions; Being a highly knowledgeable organization; and Professionalism, Transparency, Resolve, and Wisdom in Enforcing.

# CHAPTER FOUR

# THE GOOGLE INC. CASE : UNFOLDING THE WORKING OF CCI

**<u>Facts of Case</u>**

A complaint made by a businessman named Vishal Gupta caused the Competition Commission of India (CCI) (Respondent) to order an investigation into Google Inc. for allegedly abusing its dominating position in online search advertising. Gupta claims that from January 2013 to October 2013, when the account was deleted by Google, businesses owned by him had been submitting adverts in Google Adwords. The Competition Commission of India (CCI) issued an order in accordance with section on April 15, 2014.Based on the prima facie opinion, Section 26(1) of the Act orders the Director General (DG) to look into the situation. Google Inc. (Appellant) filed a request to have the investigation order recalled since it was made without providing them a chance to be heard. On July 31, 2014, the Competition Commission of India (CCI) denied the application for the following reasons:

Issues could be dealt with later once the investigation is finished, according to CCI, which initially believed that a case for investigation under Section 26 (I)'2 was made out.

In any case, the Act does not grant the CCI the right to review, making it illegal for a legal body to review or recall its orders;

The appellants filed a writ case before the Delhi High Court challenging the contested ruling because there was no statutory provision for an appeal against such an order.

**<u>Issues</u>**

1. Is the Writ Petition filed against the CCI's order directing an investigation maintainable?

2. Does the Act contain any provisions that indicate an order under section 26(1) cannot be reviewed or recalled?

3. Does the Act contain any provisions that indicate the CCI has inherent powers to recall or review its investigation orders?

### Appellant's Arguments

The appellants argued that CCI had ordered the probe without providing a hearing opportunity. CCI rejected the request to recall the order due to a lack of territorial jurisdiction. According to the appellant, who relied on the Supreme Court's decision in Competition Commission of India v. Steel Authority of India ("SAIL'*) (2010) 10 SCC 744, the deletion of Section 37 of the Act by the 2007 Amendment to the Act—which eliminated the power of review—does not imply that the power to recall an order also ends, as recall and review are distinct powers.

Although CCI had the authority to review its order prior to the 2007 Amendment, counsel for the Respondents argued that this authority had been removed with the repeal of Section 37 of the Act. The Act's structure forbids the review or recall of the directives. The Appellants would not incur any harm, according to CCI's argument, and as the inquiry was in its preliminary stages and not definitive in nature, there was no need for a hearing.

### Respondent's argument

Respondents also argued that the application was simply made to get a thorough hearing at the beginning and that it might still be considered at a later point. Significant review authority is expressly forbidden. As CCI's jurisdiction to handle a problem involves a mixed question of fact and law, any involvement with the investigation would simply cause needless delay in the procedures. Once an investigation is underway, intervention is not permitted by the Act. According to CCI, section 26(1) of the Act's application is still in the planning stages and is not subject to appeal.After examining the Act's numerous clauses and a number of decisions, the Delhi High Court reached the conclusion that the authority to recall remains regardless of whether judicial, quasi-judicial, or administrative jurisdiction is being used.

# CHAPTER FIVE

# CRITICAL ANALYSIS

The Supreme Court determined that the authority used by CCI under section 26(1) is administrative in JSPL V. SAIL (2010) 10 SCC 744. Due to the following factors, the CC's order directing an investigation, which it issued in accordance with Section 26(4) of the Act, is susceptible to review or recall even in the absence of a particular power or pro vision under the Act:

1. Under the Competition Act, an investigation by the DG does not begin simply with the receipt of a reference or piece of information; rather, it doesn't begin until the CCI has formed a preliminary belief that an Act infringement has occurred.

2. Before passing an order under section 26(1) of the Act directing the DG to conduct an investigation into the matter, the CCI must determine that there is a prima facie case of a violation of sections 3(1) or 4(1) of the Act based on the information/complaint under section 19, the reference it received from the Central or State Government, or a statutory authority, as well as its own knowledge. No investigation by the DG can be mandated without the development of such an opinion. However, according to SAIL (above), CCI is not required to hear from the person or entity that has been referred to or informed against before coming to this conclusion.

3. The law does not offer any recourse to a person or enterprise who, without being given an opportunity, has been harmed by an order or being ordered or instructed to be examined against or into pursuant to section 26(1). Although COMPAT has been established as an appeals court for CCI orders, section 53A of the Competition Act limits its appellate competence, and section 26(1) of the Act does not provide for the provision of an appeal against a CCI order. In the absence of a remedy, the aforementioned person or entity has no choice but to submit to the investigation and take part in it.

4. The DG has the same authority as a Civil Court under the Code of Civil Procedure, 1908, when trying a case in relation to I requiring the discovery and production of documents, (ii) receiving evidence on affidavit, (iii) receiving evidence from witnesses, (iv) issuing commissions for the examination of witnesses during the course of such an investigation under section 41(2) read with section 36(2) of the Act. The DG is further empowered by Section 41(3) read in conjunction with Sections 240 and 240A of the Companies Act, 1956 to examine any person under oath regarding the affairs of the person or enterprise being investigated against or into, and all officers, employees, and agents of such person or enterprise are also required to preserve all books and papers which are in the custody of the DG for a period of six months.

5. Under section 43 of the Act, it is now illegal to disobey a directive from the DG without a reasonable excuse. Up to a maximum of one crore rupees, the maximum penalty for each day of failure is rupees one lakh. As a result, it would be clear that the DG's investigative powers are much broader and more comprehensive than the Police's investigative authority under the Code of Criminal Procedure. Thus, even if the rule of audi alteram partemdoes not apply when the police are conducting an investigation under the Cr.P.C., the DG, CCI, is not subject to such a restriction.

6. As a result, the investigation by the DG and CCI is equivalent to the start of a trial or inquiry based on an ex parte prima facie opinion. Although the Supreme Court in SAIL, held that the CCI's investigation begins once the DG of the CCI has submitted a report of investigation, the Supreme Court did not have an opportunity to evaluate that the DG of the CCI has significantly more investigative authority than the Police.

7. In the absence of any statutory remedy against investigation commenced on the basis of a mere reason to suspect in the mind of the Police, writ petition under Article 226 of the Constitution of India for quashing of FIR has been held to be maintainable albeit on limited ground. Reference in this regard may be made to State of Haryana vs BhajanLal.

8. A petition against a CCI order directing an investigation under Section 26(1) of the Act would also be maintainable if the same reasoning used in cases under Article 226 for the quashing of investigations under the Code of Criminal Procedure, 1973 (Cr.P.C.) was applied. This is especially true given that the DG investigating's powers are much more broad and nearly identical to those of a civil court than the powers of the Police of investigation under the Cr.P.C. In contrast to police investigations under the

Cr.P.C., the principles of audialteram partem are applied in civil trials.

9. The availability of a hearing opportunity during CCI proceedings after the DG's report is submitted cannot always be used as a justification for denying an Article 226 remedy against the investigation's order.

10. If there is a right to approach the High Court under Article 226, such a substantive right cannot be defeated on the ground that it would cause delay.

11. The repeal of Section 37 of the Act does not prove that the legislature intended to strip CCI of its review authority. Given that the CC has the inherent authority to review and recall its orders, it's possible that the legislature omitted section 37 because it was unnecessary.

12. Nothing in the Competition Act's design suggests that the CCI is functus officio after ordering an investigation; on the contrary, as previously stated, the order of investigation is based on a preliminary one-sided view of the situation, and even if the investigation's report finds violations of the Act, the CCI is required by section 26(8) of the Act to provide the person or enterprise against which such a report has been made with an opportunity to be heard, and to do so at that time.

13. The DG, CCI's report is not legally obligatory on the CCI. It is true that the CCI must give notice before deciding whether or not there has been a violation, and it is very likely that the CCI will ultimately reject the DG, CCI report.

14. According to Section 16 of the Competition Act, the DG of the CCI is only responsible for conducting investigations; under Section 27 of the Act, the CCI is responsible for making the determination of whether any violations of the Act's provisions have occurred. (ZL) Furthermore, the DG's investigation authority is not unrestricted. When conducting the investigation, the DG, CCI is constrained by the parameters specified in the CCI's order pursuant to Section 26(1) of the Act and is not authorised to conduct a roving and fishing inquiry.This is also evident from Section 26(7) of the Act empowering the CCI to direct the Director-General to cause further investigation into the matter and from Regulation 20(6) of the Competition Commission of India (General) Regulations, 2009, empowering CCI to direct DG to make further investigation. It is thus not as if once an order under section 26(1) of the Act of investigation has been made, the investigation goes outside the domain of CCI.

# CHAPTER SIX

# CONCLUSION AND RECOMMENDATONS

According to the Delhi High Court, an investigation cannot be carried out without a prima facie opinion or in cases where one is obviously unsupportable. This decision placed a strong focus on the freedoms granted by the Indian Constitution of 1950 and came to the conclusion that investigations should not be allowed if they could result in harassment from parties. The Delhi High Court, however, stipulated that this authority must be used within particular bounds and under certain conditions in order to avoid delaying the inquiry process.

While the judgement lays out specific conditions under which CCI can review its own orders, it is a well-established legal principle that the power to review is not an inherent power. This judgement would undoubtedly encourage CCI to improve administration of its own functions as it is given flexibility to recall its orders where the circumstances warrant a modification. Before the Delhi High Court's Division Bench, CCI may appeal this decision. However, as the ruling now stands, businesses have the opportunity to use it and, in the right circumstances, contest an order mandating an investigation. This would make it easier to successfully wrap up investigations that don't reach the minimum standard established by the Act.

www.ingramcontent.com/pod-product-compliance
Lightning Source LLC
Chambersburg PA
CBHW071230140726
47996CB00004B/1558

9 798888 155547